© Copyright 2016 by CWG Publishers - All rights reserved.

This document is geared towards providing exact and reliable information in regards to the topic and issue covered. The publication is sold with the idea that the publisher is not required to render accounting, officially permitted, or otherwise, qualified services. If advice is necessary, legal or professional, a practiced individual in the profession should be ordered.

- From a Declaration of Principles which was accepted and approved equally by a Committee of the American Bar Association and a Committee of Publishers and Associations.

In no way is it legal to reproduce, duplicate, or transmit any part of this document in either electronic means or in printed format. Recording of this publication is strictly prohibited and any storage of this document is not allowed unless with written permission from the publisher. All rights reserved.

The information provided herein is stated to be truthful and consistent, in that any liability, in terms of inattention or otherwise, by any usage or abuse of any policies, processes, or directions contained within is the solitary and utter responsibility of the recipient reader. Under no circumstances will any legal responsibility or blame be held against the publisher for any reparation, damages, or monetary loss due to the information herein, either directly or indirectly.

Respective authors own all copyrights not held by the publisher.

The information herein is offered for informational purposes solely, and is universal as so. The presentation of the information is without contract or any type of guarantee assurance.

The trademarks that are used are without any consent, and the publication of the trademark is without permission or backing by the trademark owner.

All trademarks and brands within this book are for clarifying purposes only and are the owned by the owners themselves, not affiliated with this document.

Amazon FBA

Amazon FBA for Non-US Residents

Contents

Introduction 7

Chapter 1 FBA - Fulfillment By Amazon 9

    How Does It Work? 9

Chapter 2 Amazon FBA Benefits 13

    Amazon Prime 13

    Eliminates the Fulfillment Burden 14

    Provides 100% Free Return Handling and Customer Service 15

    Expedited Delivery 16

    Being Able to Leverage The Amazon Brand 16

Chapter 3 Steps To Success With Amazon FBA 18

    Amazon Seller Account 18

    Sourcing Items for Amazon FBA 19

        Retail Arbitrage Sourcing 19

        Private Label Sourcing 20

        Unique Merchandise Sourcing 21

Chapter 4 Shipping Guidelines, Supplies and Product Rules for Amazon FBA 22

    Product Rules and Guidelines 22

    Product Categories that require Amazon Approval 25

Supplies used for FBA 27

Chapter 5 Top Selling Items for Amazon FBA 30

Chapter 6 Preparing Your Amazon FBA Items for Shipment 37

    Sorting 37

    Scanning 38

    Individual Item Packing 38

    Boxing Items For Shipping 40

Chapter 7 Amazon FBA Inventory Management 42

Chapter 8 Amazon FBA for Non-US Residents 47

    Requirements for Setting up a North American Amazon Account as a Foreigner 47

    How Amazon FBA Works As A Foreign Seller 49

    Taxes 50

    Other Amazon US Requirement for Foreign Sellers 51

    Getting Paid As a Non-US Resident Amazon FBA Seller 52

Chapter 9 Critical Mistakes Every Amazon FBA Seller Must Avoid. 56

    Misunderstanding/Disregarding Sales Rank 56

    Not Taking Advantage of the Final Quarter Of The Year 58

    Failure To Reinvest For Business Expansion 59

    Stagnant Clearance Items 59

    Improper Accounting/Not Having Any Accounting At All 60

    Expanding The Business Too Quickly 61

Conclusion..63

Introduction

Amazon, ever since it started, has been providing aspiring online entrepreneurs with a means of establishing an online selling business in the United States. It has become one of the best, if not, the best online selling platform in the world.

What makes Amazon attractive to many online sellers is their FBA, or Fulfilled By Amazon program. In a nutshell, the Amazon FBA program provides sellers with services that make them focus more on growing the business, rather than the day-to-day business operations. What's even great is that now, Amazon FBA not only caters to United States residents, but also foreign sellers.

If you're a budding online entrepreneur looking for a way to break into the online selling business via Amazon FBA, this book is right for you. This book will tell you all you need to know about Amazon FBA, including how it works, how to sign-up for an account, what items you can sell and not sell, how do you send the items to Amazon's fulfillment centers, etc.

In addition, this book will also teach you everything you need to know on how to sell your items in Amazon from a foreign country. We'll talk about the fees involved, your tax responsibilities, and even how to get paid via your local bank account.

So without further ado, let's start growing your business through Amazon FBA.

Chapter 1   FBA - Fulfillment By Amazon

So you're a budding entrepreneur looking to grow your online business. You have a great product, you're busy handling all the things that make your business run; fulfilling customer orders, providing customer service, generating sales, sourcing product and trying to grow.

What if you can have a service that can make maintaining it all easier and could help you find new customers at the same time? Fulfillment by Amazon or FBA makes your products more visible to millions of loyal, happy, Amazon customers while providing the world class fulfillment, fast shipping and acclaimed customer service that can bring your business to the next level.

How Does It Work?

How does it work you ask? You simply send your inventory to Amazon state-of-the-art fulfillment centers located near your customers around the world. Your products will be stored securely and you can send Amazon as little or as much as you want. When you use FBA, your products listed on Amazon become eligible for Amazon prime and FREE Super Saver Shipping, so more of your customers can get what they want, fast and free; and more of Amazon customers can become your customers.

When customers buy your products, Amazon will pick, pack and ship them and will also manage customer service and even returns 24 hours a day. Amazon's technology works for you behind the scenes so you're free to focus on growing your business locally and globally. Not only are you continually selling, FBA will help you reach customers around the world with a click of a button.

You can even use FBA to fulfill sales from your own website and other online channels. With Amazon's ever expanding fulfillment network, your business benefits from Amazon's scale. Whether your business is small or large, FBA gives you all the tools necessary to manage your business more effectively; from pricing optimization to business analytics and personalized business recommendations.

You can manage your inventory online from any device and from any location. So the question is, do you keep doing it all yourself or use the service that can help you make more money, grow your business, save time and delight your customers.

You may be wondering what it takes to get started with Fulfillment by Amazon. It is a simple process. First, you need to create a Selling on Amazon account. Then, in Amazon Seller Central, create and convert your listings to be fulfilled by

Amazon. Choose as many products as you like and then choose to create your shipment. Next, your inventory needs to be ecommerce ready, meaning your products are labeled and packaged according to Amazon's guidelines, to create a great customer experience.

You can prepare and label your products yourself or use FBA's Label & Prep Services for a per unit fee. To simplify the process even more, if your product is new; has a bar code that can be scanned and is in a qualifying category, you can choose to commingle your inventory. This allows you to avoid the hassle of labeling and gets your products as close to the customer as possible.

Commingled products are pooled for efficiency, but tracked through the entire process to ensure a happy outcome for you and your customers. Once you're ready to send your shipment to Amazon, you can leverage your relationships with major carriers for deeply discounted shipping.

You can either send your products to fulfillment centers designated by FBA or you can use Amazon's inventory placement service to consolidate your shipments to Amazon. Now that your products are positioned close to customers, you're ready to scale with FBA.

Your offers automatically feature free two-day shipping for prime members and every shipment is backed by the Amazon

Delivery Promise. You can also use your Amazon inventory to fulfill orders from your own online store.

When you're ready to expand your reach globally, FBA has tools and expertise to help you establish your business in other marketplaces across the world. Amazon even handles customer service in your customer's local language. Use Amazon Seller Central, a web-based portal, to run your Amazon business or directly integrate your internal systems with Amazon through APIs (Application Program Interface) to automate your operations. In addition, if you ever need a hand, FBA provides tools, help content, video tutorials and other resources.

If you have any specific issues, Amazon seller support representatives are available to help 24 hours a day, 7 days a week. FBA provides a comprehensive set of tools to help you manage your inventory health, forecast customer demand, and continually improve your business performance. All this can happen from your business, your home and your mobile device. Now, you actually have time to grow your business.

Chapter 2   Amazon FBA Benefits

Many of you out there might be asking yourselves why you should take advantage of Amazon FBA. What difference does it make if you just sell your items right out of your home or your own storage facility where you don't have to pay order handling fees, pick & pack fees and weight handling fees? Well, for starters, your items would be eligible for Amazon Prime.

Amazon Prime

So, what is Amazon Prime? Basically, Amazon Prime is a paid membership for customers who purchase plenty of items on Amazon. As a customer who is a prime member, you get free two-day shipping on all of the items that you order that are prime eligible.

If you have a digital media streamer or a Smart TV, Prime can also give you access to instant streaming of movies and television shows for free. In addition, if you have a Kindle e-book reader, you can get access to a huge library of e-books that you can borrow for free.

A customer can try Amazon Prime free for 30-days. If the customer chooses to continue using Prime after the free 30-day trial, it will cost them $99 dollars per year. For some, this may look like a very expensive service. But, if you consider the free two-day shipping and if you're a customer who makes Amazon purchases frequently, that $99 dollars is a great deal. Amazon Prime customers are like the "frequent-fliers" of the online shopping world. These customers purchase more frequently than normal shoppers in Amazon.

Fulfillment by Amazon significantly increases the chance of your items to be discovered by Prime customers since FBA products are Prime eligible; FBA items feature Prime's free two-day shipping and will appear in Prime filtered item searches.

On top of that, since your items are Prime eligible, your sales will definitely increase during the holiday season. It is already a proven yearly trend that Prime customer sales increase during the holidays, since they buy presents for themselves or their loved ones.

Another benefit Amazon FBA gives you is that it relieves you of the burden of fulfilling high volumes of orders. It takes care of the packing and shipping process for you.

Eliminates the Fulfillment Burden

Let's face it, as a person who just started up his online selling business from home or a small office; you may still not have enough manpower to do the fulfillment shipping operations. It is a headache that, people who are still young at the business, often encounter. With Fulfillment by Amazon, you have the option to send your entire inventory to Amazon fulfillment centers and let them handle the packing and shipping of the items to your customers.

By sending your items to Amazon fulfillment centers, this will free up valuable time for you to meet clients and grow your business, instead of spending it packing and shipping items. In business, 100% customer satisfaction is one of the main goals to be successful. To meet that goal, you have to make sure that if a customer has any problems with your product or service, you fix it right away and you make the customer feel that they are very important.

Provides 100% Free Return Handling and Customer Service

In the business of sales, your customers will always have concerns that needs to be addressed, may it be a product issue or a service (delivery) issue. Needless to say, in order to maintain a high rate of customer satisfaction, you need to have a customer service feature that will deal with all types of problems that your customer may have. This is what Amazon FBA can bring into your business.

Amazon FBA will handle all customer service relations including all product returns with FBA orders. This is a very valuable benefit especially for sellers who aren't specialists in the customer service field. When customers order something online, they want to item to be in good condition and they want the item to reach them fast. Making fast deliveries is another benefit Amazon FBA can provide you.

Expedited Delivery

Delivery time is one factor that will sometimes make or break a sale. Customers buy items online and they want it to reach them in the shortest amount of time possible. With Amazon FBA, your items will have the benefit of faster shipping times. This faster delivery time is attributed to your items being eligible for Amazon Prime; it gives your items a free two-day delivery feature. On top of that, it will also make your items eligible for 24/7 customer service and delivery tracking.

Since the items are shipped from Amazon fulfillment centers, they process and ship quicker. This is way faster than having the item come from the seller directly. You can leverage on Amazon's proven track-record of quality customer service so you can be rest assured that shoppers can depend on helpful assistance.

Being Able to Leverage The Amazon Brand

This is where the entire concept of fulfillment by Amazon is based off of. A third-party seller such as yourself is basically leveraging Amazon's technology, process, reputation and customer base to increase your business. Amazon has established itself as a household brand that denotes excellent customer service and ease of shopping online.

Similar to franchising, Amazon FBA puts your business in line with the Amazon brand and lets you borrow Amazon's outstanding reputation. This is definitely the best benefit that you can get out of Amazon FBA, especially if you are just a small start-up business.

Chapter 3   Steps To Success With Amazon FBA

Setting up Amazon FBA is very, very easy. If you know how to navigate online and fill up forms, then setting up Amazon FBA will be a piece of cake.

In fact, the only hard part about Amazon FBA is being consistent in treating it like a business. The number one reason why some sellers fail with Amazon FBA is because they consider it as a hobby. If you consider it as a hobby, then you'll get hobby-like results. If you treat it like a business, then you'll get business results.

That is the most important thing to remember when you decide to build a business with Amazon FBA. Once you decide to go through and take your first step in building a business with FBA, you then have to get an Amazon Seller account.

Amazon Seller Account

An Amazon seller account is the first thing that you need to start with Amazon FBA. Amazon Seller Accounts are different than your normal Amazon accounts. It gives you the ability to sell different categories of items on Amazon.

It comes in two selling plans, namely the Professional and the Individual plan. It is recommended that you get the Professional Seller account which costs $39.99 a month. The Professional Seller account lets you sell more than 40 items per month, which is ideal for any entrepreneur with a startup business looking to grow.

Now that you have your Amazon Seller Account, the next obvious step would be to get the items that you want to sell through Amazon FBA. 90% of sourcing items for FBA is done via Retail Arbitrage, Private Label or Unique Merchandise.

Sourcing Items for Amazon FBA

Retail Arbitrage Sourcing

Retail Arbitrage is an item sourcing concept wherein you go to big box stores, buy different non-locally sold items that are on clearance and sell them online for a much bigger price. Clearance items sell for a very cheap price making it ideal for online reselling. You can sell these items online where there's a much bigger market and therefore will bring about a higher return of investment rate. Retail Arbitrage is the biggest, most common way to source items to sell on Amazon FBA.

Sellers who do retail arbitrage usually do it by going into a store with a bar code scanning app. This bar code scanning app, usually installed on a Smartphone, is used to scan items inside the store to see which one will sell on Amazon with a higher price point.

Private Label Sourcing

Another item sourcing concept is Private Label. It is basically having someone overseas, typically China, manufacture a product for you with your own brand name on it and sell it online as your own merchandise.

Sellers who have overseas suppliers do Private Label sourcing since they create their own listings for these types of items; it eliminates competition in a listing basis. This sourcing concept is a great opportunity to make a lot of money. However, there are two main downsides to this item sourcing concept:

It is hard to find a reliable manufacturer who will make your product and make it with good quality.

If by any chance you found a good manufacturer to work with, they require a significant upfront payment just to get the process going.

Here's a tip if ever you do decide to take Private Label sourcing: Build a good relationship with a shipper that's in the same country as your manufacturer and have them check on the quality of the items in the factory for you. This saves you a lot in travel cost since you don't have to go overseas yourself.

This also gives you a chance to develop a good relationship with an overseas shipper who will not only do quality checks for you, but also send you the items fast. Putting this into practice ensures that you develop really big product brands overtime.

Unique Merchandise Sourcing

Unique Merchandise is another item sourcing concept that exists in a market that is much less competitive. Unique Merchandise is basically "thrifting" or the procurement of used, vintage goods in good condition for reselling. The main advantage when sourcing items this way is that you save a lot of money on procurement and earn big reselling.

Chapter 4   Shipping Guidelines, Supplies and Product Rules for Amazon FBA

Amazon FBA lets you leverage on their process, technology and loyal customers to increase your business. They are putting your business in line with the Amazon brand. Just like any other business, they want to make sure that the brand stays reputable. In line with keeping the Amazon brand reputable, they have implemented rules and guidelines when selling through Amazon FBA.

Product Rules and Guidelines

The absolute, most important rule and the first thing you need to know when selling via FBA is they have a zero tolerance policy for counterfeit goods. In the event that Amazon finds that your items are counterfeit, they will not entertain any explanation on how the item was procured or if it got sent by mistake. If you send something that is counterfeit, you will get into a lot of legal troubles and potentially get banned from Amazon.com.

They are very strict about this policy, since it involves you ruining their reputation as a good and trusted online shopping brand by having them accidentally sell counterfeit goods. It is imperative that you make sure all items that you are going to send to Amazon for fulfillment is not counterfeit. If you have any suspicion that you have a counterfeit item, do not send it under any circumstances until you know for a fact that the item you have is authentic.

The second most important thing to remember is whenever you send boxed shipments to Amazon FBA, make sure that the boxes are not full of packing peanuts, shredder paper or any kind of elastic plastic wrap. Do not send items in this manner or you'll get charged with extra fees for handling.

It is very likely that this is something most sellers wouldn't think of since packing peanuts is usually fine; it seems that Amazon just doesn't want to deal with the mess. Things that are acceptable to use when packing items for FBA are bubble wraps and single long sheets of paper or newspaper.

If you are sending sharp objects for FBA, make sure that the sharp edge is covered. It must be packed in a way that there's no possibility of it sliding out. Items such as plush dolls, stuffed animals and clothing must all be poly-bagged and sealed. Heat sealing is not necessary; sticker sealed bags works just fine. Amazon will not accept it if these kinds of items are not in bags and will charge you for processing fees in handling them.

If you send in any glass items, it must be bubble wrapped and boxed. Amazon also requires the boxed glass items to pass a five-point drop test to make sure that it does not break. You are also required by Amazon to label any glass items as fragile so people will know that it requires careful handling.

When labeling the boxes to be shipped to Amazon for fulfillment, make sure that it is labeled properly. This will prevent you from losing too much money on handling fees. Amazon also offers a labeling service if you don't have the free time to do it. They will charge you 20 cents per label that they have to put on and could take an extra week to process your goods.

If you send anything to Amazon FBA that is in liquid form, make sure it is completely sealed in multiple poly-bags or heat sealed bags. This is required so that no liquid, if it leaks, can ever get out of the bag. If it's not completely sealed, Amazon will just dispose of it, no questions asked.

Those are just the basic rundown of the most important things to know about the items you are sending in for Amazon fulfillment. If you do not follow these important guidelines, they will charge you extra fees, they might dispose of your goods and you can get strikes against your account.

This book also cannot stress enough the importance of not sending any counterfeit goods or anything that you think might be counterfeit. Sending counterfeit goods is the quickest way for your account to get banned and prevent you from selling anything at all.

Product Categories that require Amazon Approval

Amazon requires sellers to obtain an approval from them if they want to sell items that belong in a specific category.

The list below shows all the categories that require approval:

- 3-dimensional products that are printed from a 3D printer
- Liquor
- Car parts and power sports (e.g. snowmobile, ATV, PWC and motorcycles)
- Self beautification products
- Health supplements and other items related to personal care
- Apparels
- Books that are collectibles
- Any kind of service that needs to be rendered
- Coins that are collectibles
- Entertainment memorabilia
- Any piece of fine art
- Gift vouchers

- Perishables
- Women's footwear, bags and eyewear
- Personally designed items
- Timepieces
- Items used for science and industry
- Items used as personal ornaments (e.g. rings, necklaces, pendants, etc.)
- Sports memorabilia
- Accessories used for Travel (e.g. Luggage, Bags, trolleys, etc.)
- Any kind of appliance
- Items used in sex (e.g. vibrators, condoms, contraceptives, supplements, etc.)
- Rented books
- Visual media (e.g. DVD, VHS, Betamax, VCDs, etc.)

The reason why Amazon requires their sellers to seek permission before listing their products under these categories is because they are improving their ways of rooting out illegal products that violate their policies. They may require you to submit certain documents or fulfill certain requirements depending on the type of product that you're going to sell. This is to ensure that their sellers and customers have a safe selling and buying experience.

There are occasions where Amazon removes a product that is already categorized as permissible. This happens whenever a product has incomplete or inaccurate product information or Amazon just plainly made a mistake of categorizing a product as restricted. You will also notice that there are some items, even though they are legal, are still prohibited by Amazon policy.

Whenever your product has been mistakenly categorized by Amazon as restricted, you should immediately contact Seller support so that they can review your product and make the required adjustments, as applicable.

Supplies used for FBA

One of the most obvious things one should have when starting a business via Amazon FBA is bubble wrap. This is necessary since you'll be doing a lot of item packing and shipping. This ensures that the item you pack, especially glass items, stays secure inside the box and will not easily break when being handled during shipping.

Newspaper is another essential item when packing goods to send to Amazon FBA. Everyone should have this and is a good substitute for plastic or bubble wraps. You can use long, multiple sheets of newspaper to firmly secure items inside the box.

A Tape gun is also useful. We all know what a tape gun does; it is used to securely close boxes for shipping to Amazon.

Invest in a good LaserJet printer. LaserJet printers are used to print the shipping labels that you will put on the boxes that you are going to ship to Amazon. For you to print labels obviously you need some blank label sheets to print the labels on; this is definitely a must-have when printing labels in-house.

Poly-bags are very important especially if you're shipping items that doesn't come in their own little individual packaging. A thing to remember about using poly-bags is that if the width of the poly-bag is more than six inches long, you are required to put a suffocation warning label on it. You can buy rolls of suffocation labels and put it on the poly-bags yourself, or you can purchase poly-bags that already have suffocation warning labels printed on them.

It is also recommended that you buy a Bar code scanner. For $30 you can get a great one off online. Buy a very simple USB based bar code scanner; this will definitely help you in scanning anything with a bar code.

This is a vital tool and the $30 that you will be investing is well worth it, otherwise, you'll going be typing those long numerical codes for your items on your number pad until the end of time. The bar code scanner makes handling and entering your items on Amazon less tedious.

You're also going to need cardboard boxes to ship your products in. You can get cardboard boxes from any Home or Office supplies store. Make sure you buy boxes in different sizes to accommodate whatever size your items come in. The great thing about shipping your items for Amazon fulfillment is that you can take advantage of their partnered shipping via UPS.

Through their partnered shipping, the percentage you pay for sending items over to Amazon is unbelievably cheap. It only cost roughly around 50 cents per pound of item weight.

Chapter 5   Top Selling Items for Amazon FBA

In this chapter we will discuss the different items that are good to start and build a business with Amazon FBA. By this time you have already familiarized yourself with the different Amazon product policies and guidelines and should be able to apply them when sourcing these items.

Most of these products will not cost you more than $5 and you can sell them at a much higher price point. This rewards you with a good amount of profit.

- *Vintage VHS tapes* – These items are very popular with vintage collectors who are into vintage flicks. You can get these items in thrift stores for 49 cents and sell them at around $15 to $18. If you can find an item that cost 49 cents and turn them into $15 to $18 dollars, then you've struck gold and should take advantage of it.

- *Small electronic devices* – Small electronic items like pedometers are great items to sell in FBA. You can get these for a buck or less and you can resell them online for $12 to $20. Another great example of these is scientific calculators made by Texas Instruments. There are still people out there who make use of or collect different kinds of scientific calculators. This is another market where the competition is less, so taking advantage of it is a must.

- *Phone cases* – More than half of the population of our planet own phones. Being that phones are essential communication devices, it is very important to keep them safe and in good working order. What better way to do that than to put them in phone cases. Phone cases protect the device from the normal wear and tear of everyday usage and sometimes from accidental mishandling. You can buy phone cases wholesale for $1 each and sell them online for around $40 dollars depending on the brand and design.

- *Digital cameras* - No, these are not the DSLR ones. These digital cameras are the small point-and-shoot kinds that are great for casual photography. Even though we have Smart phones now that have built-in HD cameras, nothing beats a dedicated device built for one sole purpose. These devices are still attractive in countries where technology doesn't progress as fast as the rest of the modern world. Due to Amazon's global reach, you can still sell these cameras and get a good amount of profit.

- *Electronic connectors, attachments and cables* – Cables are very important for any modern day electronic device. It allows you to charge the device or connect one device to another. People often lose their cables and connectors especially when traveling. Therefore, selling a wide range of connectors for different devices is a good way to make money. You can buy cables for $3 to $4 per piece wholesale, and sell them for around $20 to $30.

- *Board games* – Nothing makes get-togethers fun and enjoyable than a board game. You can buy them for $2 each and sell them online for $15 to $18. There are many types of board games to choose from such as scrabble, monopoly, trivia games and a whole lot more.

- *Puzzles* – Puzzles still have a huge cult following. There are many people who collect different types as a hobby making it a viable item for reselling on Amazon. Puzzles come in different sizes and designs. This will usually cost you about 50 cents depending on the size and design. It sells for about $8 to $20.

- *Books* – Books are another viable item to sell via FBA. There are many customers out there who love collecting them, especially if the books are hard-bound. Textbooks about different topics are also selling really well on Amazon. You can get them from any auction house, thrift store or any big box store under the used section.

Although it takes some work to find the right books to sell, it is really well worth the time and investment since you can get them for as low as 50 cents and sell them for about $100 depending on the condition and the type of the book. Even though every topic is accessible right know through global access, sometimes it helped to have something right at your fingertips. This is what makes physical books attractive.

- *Old 80's action figures* – These are great items that also appeal to action figure collectors. Through the years, action figures have become a valuable novelty item. These items are in such a high demand that some collectors are willing to pay thousands for a particularly rare item. You can get old action figures for less than a dollar and you can sell them for a higher price depending on the rarity of the item.

- *New or outdated recordable media* – These items may come in a form of a recordable DVD/CD/Cassette, etc. You can buy these items for 99 cents or less and sell them for about $8 to $20 depending upon the brand. Make sure that it is still in its original packaging.

- *Small sized items/products* – Baby accessories such as baby bottles, baby pacifiers, bibs, etc. do well because you are able to fit a large quantity of these items into boxes for shipping to Amazon FBA. Having more products shipped in a short amount of time will yield better income for you, since you are able to get a lot of items out there quickly and at a very cheap rate.

- *Vintage cameras or Polaroids* - These classic items tend to do well in FBA. Despite the emergence of the Smartphone with a built-in high resolution camera, there are still vintage photography purists out there who are always on the lookout for these types of items. The vintage item market is not very saturated; therefore selling items that cater to this market will certainly yield a great return of investment.

- *Guitar Hero guitars* – There is a huge following for the Guitar Hero series of games. Guitar Hero is a rhythm based game where you make use of a Guitar-like controller; it has several buttons that you tap in conjunction with the beat of the music. The Guitar Hero guitars come in different shapes and sizes and are very in demand by gamers.

- *Walkmans and Discmans* – Walkmans and Discmans are vintage items that you can get in any thrift store. You can buy them for about 5$ and then sell it online around $28-$62. It is unbelievable, but apparently there are people who are still interested in these items. It is very likely that the people who are still interested in these items are collectors.

- *Kids travel games* – This is a very important item for parents who are traveling across the state or across the country with their children. Children need something to do at the backseat while they are on a long trip.

When you put children in the backseat for long periods of time, they become irritable. Therefore, it is important that they do something during the duration of the trip.

This makes the whole traveling experience easy and enjoyable for both the kids and the parents. This is exactly why this item is very in demand and sells well online.

- *The Simpsons items* - The Simpsons is America's well loved animated family and it's no surprise that the Simpsons brand is still a big seller. Any item, may it be a board game, clothing, children's accessories, that has the Simpsons brand will sell well. These items will sell for about $30 to $60 dollars used on FBA. The new ones will go for more than $100.

- *Small tools* – Small tools set are very in demand by customers who does self-repair a lot. Small tool items include small screwdriver sets, torx screw sets, etc. You can buy them for about $2 to $3 per set wholesale and you can sell them online at about $7 to $10 per set.

- *Vintage gaming consoles, games and accessories* – Retro gaming is a very big thing in the gaming community. In YouTube alone, you will see thousands of collectors showcase their items to their subscribers. This shows that there is a very large market for used gaming consoles, games and its accessories. It is a well worth investment to go around thrift shops and garage sales hunting for old games and consoles that you can sell for a good price to these collectors.

These are great items to start off your Amazon FBA business. Maybe you don't have that big of a budget to bankroll your retail arbitrage efforts or maybe you just want to tread the water first before committing to it fully. Most of these items will not cost you more than $5; therefore it minimizes the risk of you losing a significant amount of money if ever something goes wrong.

You may have to wait for half-off days to get some of these items, but it is worth it considering the savings you'll get when purchasing them. These are good ideas to get your brain rolling if you're new.

It is important to remember that these items are just starting points to get your ideas rolling in the right direction about what type of items to sell. The secret is learning how to snowball it and build it up as you go along. You can literally make thousands of dollars just from these items alone as long as you build it up slowly and sell it one item after another. This is an excellent way to get your return of investments fast.

All of this takes hard work, time, a little bit of patience and consistency. This is a good place to start if you're new to FBA. Hopefully, this will get your brain to work on ideas on other potential items you could buy and sell.

Chapter 6   Preparing Your Amazon FBA Items for Shipment

In this chapter, we will discuss the step-by-step process in preparing your products for shipping to Amazon FBA. At this point you already have the different supplies needed in starting your Amazon FBA business indicated in chapter 4.

Contrary to what others may think, preparing your items for shipping to Amazon FBA is really, really easy. It is very unlikely that you'll encounter a problem with the whole process as long as you follow the proper shipping guidelines set by Amazon. With that in mind, you can start the whole process by:

Sorting

In order to prepare all the items that need to be shipped to FBA efficiently, you must first get all your items together and sort them out. A good way to do this is by segregating them by item type into boxes, so that they're very accessible when you start to enter them into your inventory in Amazon.

Another way to do this is to lay them out on a long table and organize them according to type, although you may need a bigger room to work around if you choose to do it this way.

As you segregate your items, try to multi-task and check each item individually for any damage. This will ensure that when your item gets shipped to the customer, it will not get returned as a defective item. This will definitely save you the trouble of dealing with a customer complaint and having an unsatisfied customer.

Scanning

Once you have your items segregated by type, the next thing to do is scan them with your bar code scanner and enter each item in your Amazon inventory. Once you scan your items with your bar code scanner, Amazon will automatically cross-reference the bar code with their catalogue and show you the item with its corresponding item name and SKU.

When scanning, scan your items by section. If you have all your items laid out on a long table, start from the far left going to the right until you finish entering everything into your Amazon inventory. Do the same procedure if you have your items segregated into boxes. Start with one box and then move to the next every time you finish.

Individual Item Packing

A lot of people tend to over think and over complicate this particular part of the item preparation process. Some people literally over pack the item because they worry that the item might break during transit. What happens when they over pack is that they tend to prevent the bar code from being scanned easily.

The best way to pack and prepare your items is to make use of poly-bags for items that come in their original packaging. Most packing jobs use 10 x 13 sized poly-bags for everything. You have the option of cutting them down to size depending on the item that needs to be packed. You can heat shrink them or just fold it and tape it firmly, making sure that the item doesn't move around inside the packaging.

Amazon's policy regarding packing items is you have to make sure that each individual product's bar code can be scanned from the outside of the material that you're wrapping it in. They don't want to have to rip the packaging open just to be able to scan the barcode.

For products that do not come in its original packaging, make sure to wrap them in bubble wrap and tape them securely. This applies to used electronic items such as digital cameras, calculators, etc. Another thing that you can do for products that doesn't have their original packaging is put them in a small cardboard box. This is a very important technique especially if you're shipping glass wares.

As was mentioned in the previous chapters, Amazon requires boxed items to pass a five-point drop test. Therefore, it is imperative that you make sure that you don't have any open spaces inside the box where the item has a chance of moving and breaking. The main key is to make sure that your product does not get damaged.

Brand new items that you want to ship to Amazon FBA can be shipped as is. Brand new items come in their original packaging and their own shrink wrap. The only thing left for you to do is put the Amazon barcode label over the existing manufacturer's barcode. Make sure the Amazon barcode completely covers the manufacturer's barcode so that they won't have any problems in scanning your items when it reaches the fulfillment centre.

There may be times when you have to send a brand new item that has multiple manufacturers' barcode on them. What you can do is get a blank label sticker and put them over the manufacturer's barcode. Make sure that the only visible barcode is the Amazon barcode that you print online from your Amazon inventory. As with any other item, make sure that the item is in good condition, wrap them as needed and put the Amazon barcode over the existing manufacturer's barcode.

Remember, the responsibility of making sure your product is protected and secure during shipping lies on you, not Amazon.

Boxing Items For Shipping

Once you have your items individually packed and labeled with an Amazon barcode, now you are ready to put them in the box for shipping. Make sure to use durable cardboard boxes so that they won't easily rip open during transit. Packing items in boxes is pretty self-explanatory; make sure to put larger items on the bottom and smaller items on top.

Keep the boxes filled and packed tightly weighing in at about 40 lbs to 50 lbs, as per Amazon guideline. Tape them firmly with the tape gun. Once you have done that, make sure to put the shipping plan labels on the box. Similar to the Amazon barcode label, you can print the shipping plan label from your shipping plan screen on your Amazon account.

Chapter 7   Amazon FBA Inventory Management

Managing your inventory is a very crucial step that a lot of people seem to overlook. Managing your inventory is important in making sure that you're getting the most value out of every item. This also makes sure that you're not just accumulating a bunch of clutter in Amazon warehouses, gaining a hoarder status.

A great example in managing your inventory is when you have to pull out a particular product from your inventory. There are a number of reasons why you have to pull out your product out of your inventory in FBA. One of them is when a particular product gets rightfully categorized as restricted and you can't sell them on Amazon.

Amazon's restricted product policy changes from time to time. This is completely normal. When this happens, your listing gets blocked and you can't sell that particular item on FBA. You can either get it disposed by Amazon for $0.35 per item or have it sent back to you for $0.50 per item. Most sellers prefer having their items sent back to them so that they can sell the item in another outlet.

This is one of the things that come into play that requires you to effectively manage your inventory; make sure you are updated on restrictions, pricing, inventory duration and other various factors so that you will not lose the value that you have invested on your inventory.

As a good practice, most sellers run their FBA inventory for 90 days. The reason for this is that during the course of the year, you can accumulate a lot of items extremely fast. Putting a timeframe for your items ensures that it does not accumulate too much in Amazon fulfillment centers in the event that it does not sell out.

So, for 90 days, list your items on the price that you want. If the items sells, which a lot of times it does, then that's perfect. When a product sells, you get your initial investment back and you get your profit. You then move on to the next product.

If the item doesn't sell, do a price reduction but still staying above your capital for the item. If you're selling a product for $60 with a capital price of $10 and it doesn't sell, then you may reduce the price down to $30.

This ensures that you still keep a $20 dollar margin despite reducing the price. This is a good technique to make the item move and still not incur any losses.

Some people use Amazon inventory re-pricers. What re-pricers do is that they automate the re-pricing process for your online inventory. It makes use of an algorithm that will predict the optimal price for your item and reprice them depending on the market.

Although repricers make the task of repricing much easier, some sellers choose to steer away from them due to the fact that doing a more hands-on approach and seeing how everything is going gives you better control over your inventory.

Also, check on your Amazon seller account page. Your seller account page gives you a lot of valuable information regarding the pricing of a particular inventory that you have. It shows you how close you are to the lowest price of a particular product so you can adjust the pricing accordingly.

Another thing to watch out for is when you have inventory that have expiration dates. If you're keeping items with expiration dates, make sure you keep track of them closely. If you are keeping your inventory for 90 days and your item expires in 15 days, then you'd be losing some of your investment. So, keep a close watch on your inventory and make sure to do price reductions at the right time to move items out quickly.

Twice a year Amazon does inventory cleaning. What this means is they do in-house cleaning of their warehouses to make sure that there are no stagnant items that are being kept for an extended amount of time.

Remember, Amazon does their in-house cleaning during the months of August and February. When you send in your items to Amazon FBA, they each put a birth date on those items. When they do in-house cleaning and the current date is way past than what's indicated on those items, you get charged long-term storage fees.

Long-term storage fee is a lot different than your monthly storage fee that doesn't equate much. The long-term storage fee will definitely kill your profits. So, you want to make sure that you're managing your inventory; you're staying up to date with your items and managing their prices.

Keeping up to date with your products also dictates which items you're supposed to source. You have to know which products are selling and which products are not selling so that when you go product sourcing, you know which items to get and to avoid.

Keeping up with product management is one of the most important things to ensure business growth. You need to know how much you are spending and how much you are selling. In addition, you have to know how much your profit is and which products are profitable. Keep this in mind when you're running your business. You want to be able to be profitable at all times and the only way to do this is to know what inventory is actually selling.

A lot of people let their items accumulate and stack up. If you have the space and you're keeping it in your own storage facility that is completely fine. But for sellers who don't have their own storage facility and are just relying on Amazon FBA fulfillment centers, you really have to watch your inventory.

Be mindful of your item storage timeframes in Amazon fulfillment centers. The closer you get to the 365 day range, the closer you are to getting charged with the long-term storage fees. This is something you want to avoid completely.

You can pay the $0.35 to have your stagnant items disposed of by Amazon, or have it sent back to you for $0.50 per item. Some might say $0.35 is very expensive. In actuality, it might be cheaper than paying the $0.50 and have the item shipped back to you and find out that it isn't something that you can actually sell.

Some things sell well, while some things don't sell. Everything has value to the right person but its finding that right person in the given amount of time is the issue. Constantly practicing good inventory management skills will definitely result to drastic improvements in your profit margin.

Chapter 8   Amazon FBA for Non-US Residents

As we all know by now, Amazon provides great opportunities for different brands to sell their products online. What's even greater is that Amazon does not only cater to United States residents, but also non-US residents as well.

In this chapter, we'll be talking about the specific steps you should take to sell your products in Amazon FBA without even setting foot on United States soil. We'll discuss the way a foreigner should sign-up for an Amazon Seller Account, and we'll also talk about the process of sending your products to the U.S. and getting paid.

Requirements for Setting up a North American Amazon Account as a Foreigner

Of course, just like what we discussed in the previous chapter, the first thing that you should do when you want to take advantage of Amazon FBA, is to register for a seller account. There are two types of seller accounts that you have to choose from during sign-up. The table below highlights the differences between the two:

Features	Professional Account	Individual Account
Able to add new	✓	✓

items to the Amazon catalogue		
Provides customer service handling, shipping, and fulfillment for your products with Amazon FBA	✓	✓
Ability to sell your products to the North American market, as well as Canada. Has the ability to control what and where you sell. Be able to manage your online business thru one Amazon seller account	✓	✓
Be able to utilize bulk reporting and listing from the Amazon Marketplace Web Service.	✓	✗
Shipping rate customization for items other than Software, Video, Books, Video	✓	✗

Games, DVDs, and Music.		
Be able to offer gift wrapping options and special promotions for your items (does not apply for Video Games, DVDs, Music, Books, Video, and Software)	✓	✗
Product Detail page top placement eligibility	✓	✗

As you can see from the table above, there are two types of Amazon Seller account available: Professional and Individual. If you're looking to have more options for your business, it is recommended that you sign-up for a Professional Amazon Seller Account.

How Amazon FBA Works As A Foreign Seller

- Once you sign-up for the Professional Seller account in Amazon, you will then enroll that account in the Amazon FBA program.

- Once you have finished sourcing your items and finished packing them as indicated in the previous chapters, you then have to import them to the United States. Once in the United States, have your shipper of choice deliver them to one of Amazon's many fulfillment centers. Amazon will then be the one to ship your items directly to your U.S. customers.

- Since you're enrolled in the FBA program, Amazon will be the one to handle storage for your items, customer service, returns, and picking & packing orders. All of the necessary fees indicated in the previous chapters apply.

- In case there are customer returns for your items, Amazon will then place them back in their fulfillment centers, provided that the items are still sellable. Items that are defective or damaged may only be returned to a U.S. address. Since you're a non-US seller, any defective or damaged items will automatically be destroyed by Amazon. This is definitely something that you have to factor into your processes and costs.

Taxes

Every Professional Seller, especially those with more than 50 Amazon FBA transactions within a calendar year, has to submit their tax information to Amazon. When setting up your Amazon seller account, you will go through what Amazon calls their "Taxpayer Wizard," which will give an Internal Revenue Service tax form for you to fill up.

Non-US resident sellers are still required to complete the tax form, and it is likely that the form that you will have to fill up is the W9-BEN tax form. The W9-BEN tax form means that you will be exempted from any United States tax reporting requirements. As per the law, foreign individuals are not subject to United States income tax requirements if working outside of the United States.

While you are exempted from United States tax requirements, this doesn't mean that you are exempted from any taxes that apply in your country of residence. You still have to pay the appropriate taxes for this kind of income in your home country. If you established a US-based LLC or corporation, it will be considered a business entity and therefore subject to United States income tax requirements.

So basically, the decision here is whether to create a US-based LLC or company, or maintain a foreign seller status. Make sure to talk to your lawyer or tax professional to identify the best course of action.

Other Amazon US Requirement for Foreign Sellers

When creating your Amazon US account, Amazon may ask you to provide the following:

- A valid Debit or Credit card that is eligible for international transactions
- Valid Phone number. Getting a U.S. Skype phone number or using Viber will definitely make your life a lot easier, since as of this writing, Amazon Seller support only caters to US numbers.

Getting Paid As a Non-US Resident Amazon FBA Seller

One of the stumbling blocks novice Amazon FBA sellers encounter is the fact that Amazon requires sellers to have a US bank account to process their payments. Bitcoin is not an option. Nor Paypal.

Since you're a non-US resident, setting up a US bank account without traveling to the United States is impossible, either as a business, or as an individual. Even if you set up your own US-based company or LLC, you still have to go to the bank personally to open a business account.

The good news, however, is that Amazon has what's called an ACCS, or Amazon Currency Converter for Sellers. The ACCS is Amazon's own system for making international deposits to foreign bank accounts. With ACCS, you can get paid directly in your local bank account, and already converted into your local currency. You don't have to worry about bank restrictions or international deposit fees.

However, not all countries support ACCS. Look below for the list of countries supported by ACCS by Amazon:

Country	Currency
Eurozone: Belgium, Estonia, France, Greece, Italy, Lithuania, Malta, the Netherlands, San Marino, Slovenia, Austria, Cyprus, Finland, Germany, Ireland, Latvia, Luxembourg, Monaco, Portugal, Slovakia, Spain	EUR
United Kingdom	GBP
Albania	ALL
Australia	AUD
Brazil	BRL
Switzerland and Lichtenstein	CHF
Colombia	COP
Denmark (including the Faroe Islands and Greenland)	DKK
Croatia	HRK
Indonesia	IDR
India	INR
Japan	JPY
South Korea	KRW

Sri Lanka	LKR
Mexico	MXN
Norway	NOK
New Zealand	NZD
Pakistan	PKR
Romania	RON
Sweden	SEK
Thailand	THB
Turkey	TRY
South Africa	ZAR
United States	USD
Argentina	ARS
Bulgaria	BGN
Canada	CAD
China	CNY
Czech Republic	CZK
Hong Kong	HKD
Hungary	HUF
Israel	ILS
Jordan	JOD

Cambodia	KHR
Laos	LAK
Morocco	MAD
Malaysia	MYR
Nepal	NPR
Philippines	PHP
Poland	PLN
Russia	RUB
Singapore	SGD
Taiwan	TWD
Vietnam	VND

Chapter 9   Critical Mistakes Every Amazon FBA Seller Must Avoid

Making your Amazon FBA business successful requires diligence, patience and sometimes pure luck. Running a business is never easy and beginners are bound to make mistakes one way or the other. Mistakes are part of the learning process, and it is through those mistakes that you'll be able to have a stronger foundation for your business. A strong foundation is an essential part in growing a business.

Therefore, it is important that we recognize and identify the most common mistakes that happen in a business. By doing this, you can make sure that the road to your business goals remain obstacle-free and at the same time learned. With that in mind, here are the most common Amazon FBA mistakes to avoid:

Misunderstanding/Disregarding Sales Rank

One of the most common mistakes rookie sellers make is completely misunderstanding Amazon's sales rank. A lot of you might ask: "What is a sales rank?" Well, in a nutshell, it is a number that is visible on the product's description that determines an item's popularity. One could also put it as the timeframe in which a particular item is last sold.

An hour after a new item is sold; its rank value will start to increase. Once another customer buys that product, its rank value significantly drops and will begin to increase again after an hour. The longer the timeframe in between each sale, the higher the rank will go.

So, with that in mind, if an item is popular it will sell fast and the sales rank value will remain low. If an item is not popular and is not selling quite well, the sales rank will increase, since the time between each sale is longer.

Most rookies make the mistake of sourcing items that have a high sales rank, not realizing that the higher the value, the more unpopular an item is and makes it difficult to sell.

Some rookie sellers disregard sales rank altogether. Not knowing the sales rank of an item is like buying a merchandise without knowing if it has good quality or not. As what most veteran FBA sellers indicate, an item having a sales rank of 250,000 or less are items that you can completely sell within a month. Items that have a rank of 60,000 or less can be completely sold within 2 weeks.

Remember, sales ranks differ from category to category. There is a big chance that a particular sales rank that sells for a particular amount of time in one category, may not apply with another category. So, it is highly recommended that you do the necessary product and inventory management needed to keep track of the different factors that affect item sales.

Not Taking Advantage of the Final Quarter Of The Year

This is another rookie mistake a lot of sellers make. We all know that sales skyrocket during the last quarter of the year. The high sales percentage is attributed to family members buying gifts for their relatives and loved ones during the holiday season.

Unfortunately, some sellers fail to capitalize on this increased sales trend; they fail to plan ahead. As early as the 3rd quarter of the year, you should already be outsourcing for products that sell well during the holidays. Some examples of items that do well during the holidays are:

- Toys
- Baby Products
- Gourmet & Grocery Food
- Electronics
- Video Games
- Clothing
- Food
- Books

- Gift Cards

Failure To Reinvest For Business Expansion

Some sellers make poor business decisions, and this is one of them. Whenever you make any kind of profit from your initial investment, it is always a good idea to reinvest that profit and grow your business. Unfortunately, some people just treat Amazon FBA as a hobby.

As was mentioned in the previous chapters, the hardest part about Amazon FBA is keeping that level of consistency in treating FBA as a business. Treat FBA as a hobby, and you will get hobby results. Treat is as a business, and you'll get business results.

Reinvesting is the key to success when starting out small. Try your best to resist the urge to celebrate early and splurge your hard earned profits. Always keep your focus; always keep your eye on the goal.

Stagnant Clearance Items

This particular mistake falls under poor product and inventory management skills. Sellers sometimes get overly excited when they see something on clearance, thinking that it will sell great on Amazon. They go out and source these items from big box stores under the clearance section, but fail to ship them out quickly.

This is a quick way to lose your investment. You have to keep in mind that all items, especially clearance items, depreciate. Clearance items are on clearance for a reason. They may be outdated, defective or maybe there's just no demand for it. It is, therefore, extremely important to make the necessary research first, before you buy items on clearance.

See if the sales rank of the item indicates that it is a fast selling product. If it is not a fast selling product, try to see if the sales rank falls within the acceptable standards of the business, whether the item is still sellable, or if you will incur losses when the price drops lower than your initial investment by the time you sell it.

As a rule of thumb, always manage your inventory diligently. Move your clearance items quickly. If you have clearance items in your inventory that is stagnant, blow it out by doing price reductions. Sell them with the same rate as your investment if you have to. This is an acceptable practice as long as you don't incur losses and as long as you get the amount of money that you have in those items.

Improper Accounting/Not Having Any Accounting At All

Though this may not be a common mistake as the ones previously mentioned, it is still important enough to be mentioned here. Having a means of efficiently tracking all business related expenses is crucial to business success.

Most often than not, beginners in the business tend to disregard small business related expenses. Whether its buying a roll of bubble wrap for packing, a pair of scissors for cutting or a single box for shipping, it is important to jot all these small expenses down.

Why? Because these expenses stack up overtime. And since these are small expenses, they are easy to lose track of. The next thing you know, you're not getting enough profits because your business expense is so large that your profit just barely covers for it.

There are many accounting software available out there that will help you in making sure that there's no expenses left untracked. QuickBooks is an example of good accounting software. It has features that allow you to track every item purchase you make, how much you have invested on those items and what's your projected profits from those items.

Invest in good accounting software and it's a guarantee that you will definitely feel the benefit it brings into your business.

Expanding The Business Too Quickly

People who are beginners in the business always commit this mistake and don't even realize it. This happens when sellers get themselves too hyped up about the success that they're having with the business.

Establishing a business, how to run it successfully and make money is not such a bad thing. This is true especially if you've mastered the principles behind it. It's never a bad thing to aim high. But, most of these sellers are new. They are building their business very quick. They are going into several different things at once, spending thousands and thousands of dollars. They put money everywhere.

The problem with this is that they can never really keep an eye on everything all at once. As a beginner, they are not yet that organized. They expand too fast and since they can't keep up with the exponential growth of the business, they lose a lot of money.

So, it is important to remember that whatever degree of initial success that comes your way, always take your time and approaching things gradually. Do not make impulse decision; do not rush head-on. Take things nice and slow and surely your business will flourish. Always keep an eye on your goal. Make sure you are always on track; stay focused.

Amazon FBA is definitely a great platform to build your business upon. You already have the essential tools necessary to make money with it and all you have to do is capitalize on the techniques described in this book and surely you'll be on your way to becoming a great online seller.

Conclusion

Selling products online via Amazon FBA is definitely a viable, long-term source of income. As long as Amazon customers exist, you'll be able to leverage the Amazon brand and push your business to success.

Thank you for purchasing this book, and we hope that the knowledge that are contained within this book has helped you understand what Amazon FBA really is, how you can leverage the Amazon brand in growing your business, and the mistakes that you have to avoid in order to make your business a success.

Thank you and may your business continually prosper.

If you're interested in learning more about how to be in tune with today's market and be able generate additional or new sources of income, we'd love to have you join our mailing list:

<Join Our Exclusive Group Here>

www.ingramcontent.com/pod-product-compliance
Lightning Source LLC
Chambersburg PA
CBHW070355190526
45169CB00003B/1022